Who'd Believe JOHN COLTER?

BY MARY BLOUNT CHRISTIAN
ILLUSTRATED BY LASZLO KUBINYI

MACMILLAN PUBLISHING COMPANY   NEW YORK
MAXWELL MACMILLAN CANADA   TORONTO
MAXWELL MACMILLAN INTERNATIONAL
NEW YORK   OXFORD   SINGAPORE   SYDNEY

To

AUNT BESS BLOUNT,

with love

Juv
F
592.7
.C65
C47
1993

Text copyright © 1993 by Mary Blount Christian
Illustrations copyright © 1993 by Laszlo Kubinyi

First edition
Printed in the United States of America
1   3   5   7   9   10   8   6   4   2
The text of this book is set in 14 pt. Cochin.
The illustrations are rendered in pen and ink.

Library of Congress Cataloging-in-Publication Data
Christian, Mary Blount.
Who'd believe John Colter? / Mary Blount Christian ; illustrated by Laszlo Kubinyi. — 1st ed.
p.   cm. Includes bibliographical references. Summary: Examines the life of the nineteenth-century woodsman John Colter and describes his experiences accompanying the Lewis and Clark Expedition and, later, as an explorer on his own. ISBN 0-02-718477-3 1. Colter, John, ca. 1775–1813—Juvenile literature. 2. Explorers—West (U.S.)—Biography—Juvenile literature. 3. Trappers—West (U.S.)—Biography—Juvenile literature. 4. West (U.S.)—Description and travel—To 1848—Juvenile literature. 5. Lewis and Clark Expedition (1804–1806)—Juvenile literature. [1. Colter, John, ca. 1775–1813. 2. Explorers. 3. Lewis and Clark Expedition (1804–1806)] I. Kubinyi, Laszlo, ill. II. Title.   F592.7.C65C47 1993   978'.01'092—dc20   [B]   92-33822

SOURCES

The American Frontier: Pioneers, Settlers and Cowboys, 1800–1899. New York: Smithmark Publishers, 1992.

Bakeless, John. *The Adventures of Lewis and Clark.* New York: Houghton Mifflin, 1962.

Barnard, Edward S., ed. *The Story of the Great American West.* Pleasantville, NY: Reader's Digest Press, 1977.

Beck, Warren A. and Ynez D. Haase. *Historical Atlas of the American West.* Norman, OK: University of Oklahoma Press, 1992.

Blumberg, Dorothy Rose. "Colter's Hell." In *Whose What?* New York: Holt, Rinehart & Winston, 1969.

The Book of the American West. New York: Bonanza Books, 1963.

"The Early Frontiers." In *The Old West,* edited by George Constable. New York: Time-Life Books and Prentice Hall, 1990.

Eggelston, Edward. "A Foot Race for Life." In *Stories of American Life and Adventure.* New York: American Book Company, 1891.

Erdoes, Richard. "Run for Your Life, White Man." In *Tales from the American Frontier.* New York: Pantheon Books, 1991.

Harris, Burton. *John Colter: His Years in the Rockies.* New York: Charles Scribner's Sons, 1952.

Hoetzman, William H. and Glyndwn Williams. *The Atlas of North American Exploration.* New York: Prentice Hall, 1992.

The Journals of Lewis and Clark. Edited by Bernard DeVoto. New York: American Heritage Publishing Co., 1963.

Lamar, Howard R., ed. *The Reader's Encyclopedia of the American West.* New York: Thomas Y. Crowell, 1977.

Line, Les. "In Praise of Weeds." *American Heritage,* Vol. XXI, No. 6, pp. 102–106.

The Native Americans: The Indigenous People of North America. New York: Smithmark Publishers, 1992.

Otfinoski, Steven. *Lewis and Clark Leading America West.* New York: Ballantine Books, 1992.

Reynolds, Lindor. *Forts and Battlefields of the Old West.* New York: M & M Books, 1991.

"Trailblazers and Trappers." In *American Folklore and Legend,* edited by Jane Polley. Pleasantville, NY: Reader's Digest Press, 1978.

CONTENTS

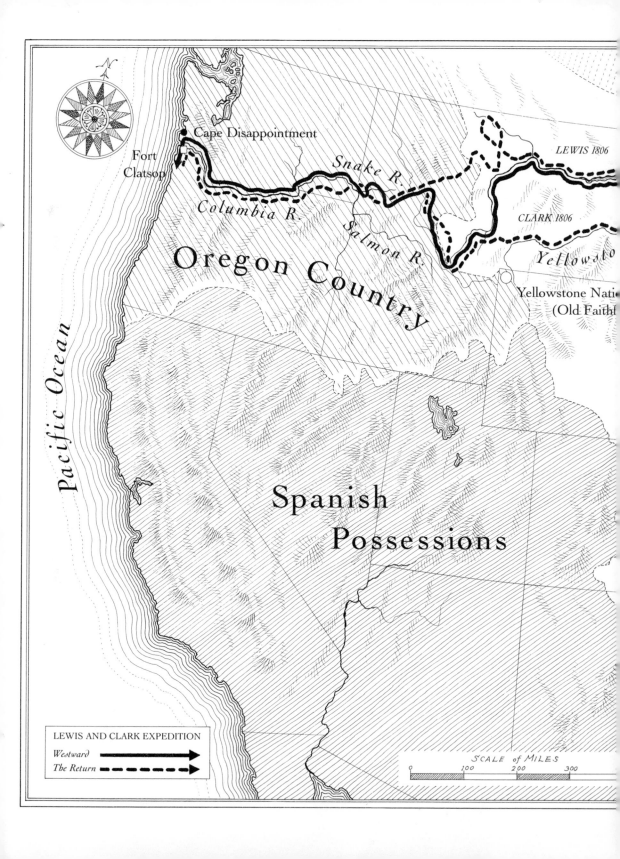

Cape Disappointment

Fort
Clatsop

Snake R.

Columbia R.

Salmon R.

LEWIS 1806

CLARK 1806

Yellowsto

Yellowstone Nati
(Old Faithf

Oregon Country

Pacific Ocean

Spanish

Possessions

LEWIS AND CLARK EXPEDITION

Westward

The Return

SCALE of MILES

0   100   200   300

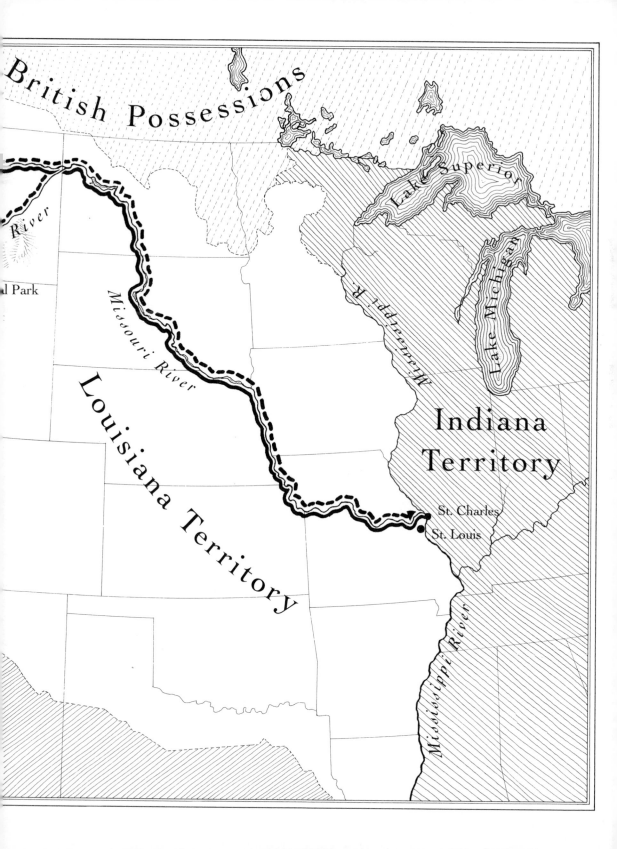

British Possessions

Lake Superior

Lake Michigan

Mississippi R.

Indiana
Territory

St. Charles

St. Louis

Missouri River

Louisiana Territory

River

d Park

Mississippi River

One THE WRONG SIDE OF THE MOUNTAINS

JOHN COLTER KNELT quietly behind the trunk of the big pin oak. The underbrush not ten yards ahead rustled. He could feel the hair on the back of his neck standing straight up like that of a riled dog.

What was it? A black bear? Maybe a mountain lion? He let his fingers slide slowly down the long barrel of his rifle to the trigger.

Sweat popped out above his lip, and his heart thumped against his rib cage. Slowly he raised the rifle until its sight was even with his keen blue eyes and the butt was against his shoulder. He tried to steady his breathing. Quiet, quiet, he thought. Slow. Don't hurry.

It wouldn't pay to fire without a clear, well-defined

target. He didn't want to wind up striking another hunter, or only wounding an animal that might turn on him. Besides, loading a rifle took too long to waste a ball on thin air. His daddy had taught him that.

Paw had stood the long rifle on its butt and told John to stand next to it. "When the top of your head is even with the top of the barrel, I'll teach you to hunt," he had promised. After that John had spent many a winter evening near the hearth of their cabin with Paw watching over his shoulder while John practiced cleaning and loading everything except the ball itself.

"No, sir!" Maw had put her foot down on that. "Don't you go arming that boy in the cabin! Why, he'll wind up shooting a hole in the wall or in my good feather bed!"

So John had practiced the rest of it until it had become routine: He would set the rifle on the ground, butt down, and cradle it with his arm so that he could look right down its barrel. He'd get out the cow's horn of gunpowder that hung from his belt. He'd measure into his cupped hand enough black powder to cover a small metal ball and pour it into the barrel. Then, from the box carved into the wooden butt of his rifle, he'd get out a metal ball and a patch of cloth sticky with bear grease, put the patch on the barrel hole, and put the ball on top of the patch. Next he'd unsnap the ramrod from its nest on the rifle and ram the ball down the barrel as far as it would go. He'd return the ramrod to its place and open the pan, get out the powder once more, pour a small amount into the pan, close it, cock—and fire. Then it had to be done over again.

No, sir, it didn't pay to waste a shot, and John never did. That was why he was probably the best shot in the state of Virginia for his age, which was ten or thereabouts.

Calendars weren't a strong point in his family, but people said he was born sometime around 1775, the year before Virginia was declared a state and the war for independence began. It had been only two winters now since the British had finally agreed to a cessation of arms. His parents had been born British citizens, but they'd never thought of themselves as anything but Americans first and Virginians second.

The bushes parted a bit. John closed his left eye and with his right looked straight down the barrel, lining up the two sights, and waited. Out stepped a little black-and-white skunk. Startled, John Colter took a step back and tripped over a tree root. His finger tightened on the trigger. *Bam!* The ball exploded from the rifle and struck a low-hanging branch of a birch tree, snapping it in two. It swung down, shaking the bushes where the critter was standing.

The terrified skunk used its only defense and sprayed its foul-smelling liquid in John's direction before trotting off safely into the brush.

"Phew!" John yelled. His eyes stung and immediately teared. He leaped over fallen logs and dodged low-hanging

branches as he raced blindly for home, yelling, "Maw! Maw!"

His dog, Buck, loped giddily toward John, his whole body wagging. Buck stopped abruptly, his nose quivering. Yelping, he tucked his tail between his legs and skittered into the brush.

"Johnny Colter!" Maw said from the door of their cabin. She was holding her nose, so her voice sounded as twangy as a mouth harp. "Don't you dare come in this cabin smelling like something even Buck won't have anything to do with. Take this lye soap and get yourself down to the creek right now."

Ellen Shields Colter followed her son at a safe distance with his other pants and a shirt of dove-gray flannel. John removed his clothes, and his mother, using a forked branch, swung them over a tree limb.

Joseph Colter came running up, his rifle at the ready. "What is it? What—" Since Paw was coming from downwind, John knew his father would find out what was the matter quickly enough.

"It'll be months before we can get near those clothes again without our eyes watering," Paw said, shaking his head. "I reckon the emergency's over. I best get back to the cornfield—the plow's waiting." A twinkle of laughter danced about his eyes. "I reckon our boy won't stalk a skunk again anytime soon."

Maw leaned against a tree. "Let's just hope the wind

won't change directions, or the smell will follow us home. It's enough to scare the hens from laying."

"What am I gonna do, Maw?" John asked. "I don't think it's coming off."

"Well, I reckon we'll just have to put up with you for a time," she said. "We can't exactly put you out on a tree limb with your clothes, can we? But it's warm. You can sleep outside till the smell wears off some." She sighed. "Just what were you doing out battling a polecat, anyway, Johnny Colter? And where are the fish you were supposed to catch for tonight's supper?"

John smiled. He knew he could make Maw laugh at one of his tall tales and forget about that stinky old skunk. And she'd forget that he had been out playing frontiersman when he should've been fishing. "I caught a whole heap of fish, Maw. Big 'uns!" John spread his arms wide to show the size. "I caught so many that I could've fed our whole family and all the families in Virginia."

"Oh, and just where are all these fish?" she asked, eyeing him suspiciously. "I reckon you're gonna tell me a big black bear stole 'em from you."

John laughed. He hadn't thought of that. Big bear. He'd have to remember that one. "No, Maw, but I caught a whole lot. Without all those fish taking up a lot of room, the river's water level dropped down to just a little trickle. There I was with a canoe full of fish just begging to be fried. But my canoe was sitting all high and dry in the middle of the creek bed. Why, I had to throw those fish back just so's I could float my canoe to shore."

Maw threw her hands into the air and clicked her tongue against the roof of her mouth. *"Tʃk tʃk."* She laughed. "Johnny Colter, what am I going to do with you? You are such a prevaricator."

"What's that, Maw? What's a preee-var-i-ca-tor?"

"That's a *liar,* Johnny Colter. A plain old liar. You are worse than any of those mountain men who come into Staunton telling their tall tales. If you don't quit your joshing, nobody will believe a thing you say."

John kept on scrubbing; he didn't say anything back to Maw. But he knew there was nothing bad about those mountain men. Why, everybody told about that one fella—Daniel Boone was his name—and how he'd wrestled bears and lived with the Indians and all. When John grew up, he wanted to be just like him.

Ellen Colter shrugged wearily. "When you're dried off, rub yourself with these green pine needles. Maybe it'll help cover the smell some."

She headed back to the cabin, leaving John to keep scrubbing away the smell of skunk. When he was satisfied that he had removed as much of the smell as he could, he crawled onto the bank. Then he sat staring at the hazy blue mountain range to the west.

He felt downright crowded with the mountains strung out to the west and settlers pushing in from every other

direction. Why, it had gotten so that a body couldn't walk more than ten miles in any direction without seeing another human being or the chimney smoke of a cabin. It was hard to breathe with so many folks pressing so close.

John slipped into his clean clothes, then glanced once more at the mountains before he headed for home. What was on the other side of those mountains? Someday, when he was a grown-up man, he would find out for himself.

Two

THE OTHER SIDE OF THE MOUNTAINS

JOHN GREW TALL and lean and muscular. His face was bronzed by the sun and wind so that he was as brown as any Indian. Only his clear blue eyes and the pale skin beneath his buckskins gave evidence to his origins. He spoke softly and had a way of looking a person in the eye that earned respect.

John left home when he was about eighteen years old, when he'd gotten just plumb tired of looking at the backside of a plow and mule. For ten years he roamed the woods and lived off whatever he and nature could provide. He learned the ways and languages of the Indians he met. This made him strong and willing to endure hardship. His slender frame belied the strength he had developed. More than once he was compared to his idol, Daniel Boone.

The air was crispy cool in October of 1803. In his baby-soft buckskin clothes, which had been darkened by smoky camp fires and stained by the bear grease he used to ward off insects, John strode along the wooden sidewalks of Louisville, Kentucky.

Only occasionally did he glance at those who gawked at him. With his forty-four-inch Kentucky rifle resting on his shoulder, John Colter attracted attention even in Louisville, the other side of the mountains, where the sight of rugged frontiersmen strolling down the main street was as common as pig tracks. Of course, he figured, that might have been because he hadn't shaved in a month of Sundays, and it had been longer than that since he'd bathed. He might be smelling a bit ripe by now.

Crimson autumn leaves swirled about the sidewalks as John walked purposefully toward the little weathered gray clapboard building down the street. Word had spread like a windswept brushfire that a man named William Clark, a captain in the United States Army, was looking for woodsmen. "He's heard about you, John Colter, and he's particularly interested in talking to you," a fellow woodsman, Jake Peabody, had told John a couple of weeks before when they'd met on a trail.

The bell above the door jangled when John Colter stepped inside the plain room, bare except for a fancy map that hung on one wall and a single desk and two straight-backed chairs. A red-haired man sat behind the desk, writing. He looked up when John entered. Standing to offer his hand, the man said, "I'm Captain William Clark, U.S. Army, co-captain to Captain Meriwether Lewis. Who might you be, sir?"

John offered his hand to the captain. "John Colter, Captain. I heard you wanted to see me."

Captain Clark motioned to the extra chair, and John sat. The captain nodded toward the map on the wall. John followed his gaze.

"Captain Lewis was appointed by President Jefferson to recruit men for the Corps of Discovery," Captain Clark said. "And Captain Lewis selected me to be his co-captain. We are looking for a special breed of men, men like you, John Colter. I have watermen, men experienced in navigating rough waters. I have cooks, carpenters, a translator, and a blacksmith. But what I need now are men who can feed us, hunters who are sure shots, strong and long enduring."

John twitched uncomfortably in the chair. He was more used to sitting on the ground or on a fallen log. "I'm tough as a mule," he told the captain. "I can outrun a deer, outjump a rabbit, outfight a bear, and outclimb a squirrel. I can track a tiptoeing Indian over nothing but rock and smell a mountain lion a mile away. And as for shooting, I can knock the shell off a snail without touching his scrawny little body."

Captain Clark laughed jovially. "And you can spin a tale taller than a loblolly pine."

He stood up and leaned forward, looking straight into John Colter's blue eyes. "Let me tell you about this mission straight out so that you won't be misled by any rumors that might be spreading around Louisville. President Jefferson has bought from the French emperor Napoleon all the land drained by the Mississippi River and its tributaries. Until we've taken a look at it, we don't know just how much land that is." He walked over to the wall map and spread his fingers across it. "President Jefferson wants to see if it's worth what he paid, or if the U.S. of A. now owns nothing more than a pig in a poke."

West of the Mississippi! John could feel his pulse quicken and his skin prickle. He'd come to the other side of the mountains. Now was his chance to go to the other side of the big river—and to be paid for it!

"I need stout, hearty, unmarried young men who are accustomed to the woods," Clark said.

John nodded, understanding. They didn't know what to expect out there in unexplored territory, so they didn't want to take men who had families. There was always a chance that they wouldn't come back.

"We don't know yet how far west this land goes," Clark said. "But we do know that the Missouri River empties into the Mississippi. The Spaniards have explored the Missouri up as far as Three Forks, where they found a village of Mandan Indians. But that's about as far as they got before they were forced by bad weather and dwindling supplies to turn back. There are a handful of mountain men who trap along there, too. They've reported the Mandans are friendly, so that won't be any trouble. And there's a sea captain by the name of Gray who found a river every bit as wide as the Missouri emptying into the Pacific Ocean. He named it Columbia.

"We don't know for sure, but we think the Columbia River may connect with the Missouri, or be no more than a day's land travel away," Clark said. He walked back around his desk and sat again. He struck his desk with his fist. "Think what that will mean, man! If we can follow these rivers all the way to the Pacific Ocean, we will have found the water gate to the Orient. It was Columbus's dream. We can make it come true. And we will be the first men to go clear across the continent. We may meet people who have never before laid eyes on fair-skinned folks. We may see animals and plants and people that nobody this side of the Mississippi has ever seen."

John swallowed hard, thinking of the possibilities. He had to go, whatever the risks, whatever the cost.

Clark sat back down. "Your reputation is enough for me, Colter." He shoved a paper and a quill pen toward John. "If you want the adventure of a lifetime, sign here."

John looked at Captain Clark. "I can read the wind and tell when a storm's coming before the sky has a cloud in it. I can read the grass and know how long it's been since a deer passed that way. But I can't read writing."

Captain Clark nodded. "It says that you sign on with the United States Army as a private. That you will faithfully serve the Corps of Discovery. That you will obey all orders given by your superiors."

John frowned. He was a loner, a wanderer. And he felt that no man was his superior. But if he went with this red-haired dreamer, he would see things undreamed of. John took the quill and carefully printed his name, the only words he knew how to write.

Captain Clark sent John to join Captain Lewis and the other members of the Corps of Discovery in Saint Louis, in the Missouri Territory, the "jumping-off place" where the Missouri and Mississippi rivers met. Winter had set in, and Captain Lewis and Captain Clark had established a place they called Camp Wood. There John gradually became acquainted with those who would be his companions on the journey west.

George Droulliard, a fellow woodsman, had done some trapping west of the Mississippi and was an expert on universal sign language. He was having as hard a time as John at taking orders from someone else. More than once, the two of them were fined part of their pay or confined to quarters as punishment for disobeying orders.

Charles Floyd said his father had soldiered with Captain Clark's older brother, George Rogers Clark. Floyd was so popular that the men elected him sergeant.

Patrick Gass was a good man, too, and also popular with the men. John Potts was a mountain man, like John.

Then there was the Frenchman, LaBich; the blacksmith, Shields; and the soldiers Shannon, Bratton, Gutherich, Whitehouse, McNeal, and Ordway. For the most part, privates' first names didn't mean much in the corps, so John didn't bother learning them. Except for Captains Lewis and Clark and Sergeants Floyd and Ordway, all the men were privates. Scots, Gaelic, French, Dutch, and Welsh were spoken along with English, but somehow the men understood enough to work well together.

Now, Peter Cruzatte was an interesting one, John thought. The son of a French trapper and a Shawnee mother, he was blind in one eye and nearsighted in the other. He'd been included only because he was a pretty good cook. And maybe because he played a mean fiddle, which helped the men while away the time stomp-dancing or just listening to the twangy music. But when Cruzatte had a gun in his hands, John preferred to be behind him, never in front of him.

There was also York, Captain Clark's black servant. He was as smart as a whip and as strong as he was tall, and he made the men laugh even when they were too tired.

And when John was counting the corps, he couldn't forget Captain Lewis's Newfoundland dog, Scannon. He was a good-natured animal, a gentle giant with a fierce look.

Captain Clark, the oldest of them at thirty-three, was a big, hearty man who was cheerful all the time. Yet he could be as straight-talking as he needed to be when one of the privates went out night-roaming and got back to camp late. And he didn't take any argument from them, either.

Captain Lewis kept more to himself. John often found him deep in a book or just staring off into space as if unaware that others existed.

John was restless, as were the other men. Waiting for winter to be done with was hard. To keep in shape, the men wrestled and had races, which John won every time.

John kept an eye on the supplies that were slowly coming in from the army depot at Harpers Ferry. Almost daily, supplies arrived—barrels of gunpowder, cloth for the gunpowder patches, and plenty of metal for the blacksmith to make into musket balls. There were twenty-one bales of beads, ribbon, looking glasses, tobacco, and coats to give to the Indians they would surely meet along the way. Nearly 4,000 pounds each of pork and flour, 2,000 pounds of cornmeal, 750 pounds of salt, 600 pounds of grease, and 560 pounds of biscuit were lined up along the dock to be loaded onto the boats, once the boats were completed.

Captain Lewis passed out flannel uniforms for the men, which John Colter didn't much take to, although he thought the red flannel long johns were good protection from the cold winter's blasts. Reluctantly, John packed away his buckskins and put on the cloth breeches and shirt.

The carpenters built a fifty-five-foot keelboat decked

fore and aft with walkways on each side. At midship they built a cabin and rigged the boat with a square sail to use when the wind was coming from a direction that would move them forward. They would be traveling against the current, which would be pretty fierce.

At the front of the keelboat they installed a big gun that could swivel in any direction. It could fire nails and other scrap iron with which they loaded it.

Under Captain Clark's direction, the men practiced walking back and forth along the walkways and thrusting long poles against the bottom of the river to push the boat forward. They also attached long ropes to both sides of the boat, in case the river bottom was too deep for the poles. Holding the ropes, the men could walk along the shoreline and pull the boat.

They also built a flat-bottomed boat called a bateau, on which they could carry many supplies. It was so large that it would need twenty oarsmen.

They built a couple of pirogues, too, which were made by hollowing out trees. The men nailed a flooring about thirty feet long and twelve feet wide between them.

Captain Lewis had the men load the big keelboat with the supplies, then lower the boat into the water. He wanted to see if they knew how to balance a load properly. They didn't! Those who could swim had to scramble into the water to save the boxes and barrels that had shifted and fallen in.

At last the snow flurries of winter turned into the nagging rains of spring. Then yellow trilliums, lemon-scented flowers, burst forth through the mud. The snow in the mountains melted and ran into the rivers, making them overflow their banks and deposit trees and debris that would have to be cleared before the Corps of Discovery could get under way.

"Soon," Captain Lewis would reply whenever John asked when. "Soon."

Everything they could do had been done. The mountain man was restless. As the rain beat against the roof of their quarters, the corps gathered and listened to John spin tall tales.

"Once I invited a traveler to share my camp fire and grub," John told them. "Old Micah was his name. Well, Old Micah had a full mouth of store-bought teeth, and when night came Old Micah took out his teeth and put them next to his bedroll.

"I was awakened sometime in the middle of the night by a stirring of pine needles. Thinking it was a hostile savage, I of course grabbed my long rifle, which was loaded and at my side." He paused.

"And what was it, John?" Peter Cruzatte asked. "Was it a savage?"

John looked from one anxious face glowing golden in the light of the hearth fire to the other, his eyes twinkling with mischief. "No, sir, it was a little bitty old pack rat, and it grabbed those false teeth and took off with 'em, leaving Old Micah a big old pecan, since they always pay for what they take, you know."

The men laughed. "Bet Old Micah was madder than a wet hen for losing his teeth," Peter said.

"Yes, sir," John said. "He ran on off to a nearby town, hoping to find himself a dentist that could make him another set. But you know, it wasn't more than a day or two before I saw that very same pack rat a-sitting on a hollow log."

"Go on, now," George Droulliard said. "How'd you know it was the same one?"

John took a deep breath and leaned back, crossing his arms over his chest in satisfaction. "Because there was this pack rat a-grinning up at me with the prettiest set of teeth you ever did see."

"John Colter, you're joshing us," Droulliard said. "Ain't nobody gonna believe a thing you say!"

The men burst into a peel of laughter, which was interrupted only by Captain Lewis's entrance.

"Get some sleep, men," he said. "We leave tomorrow."

Three GOING AGAINST THE CURRENT

THE RAIN STOPPED about noon the next day, May 3, 1804, and the men climbed aboard the pirogues, the bateau, and the keelboat and shoved off at about four that afternoon. They had expected that the Missouri River, which most folks called the Big Muddy, would be a problem, and it was. Sandbars and floating debris constantly threatened to overturn or even destroy the boats.

John Colter concerned himself little with the doings on the river, though. By day he followed along the shore with the other hunters, hunting enough game to feed the corps. Then at night he'd sit and listen to the men's complaints about the treacherous river.

On August 18 the corps celebrated Captain Lewis's

birthday. Two days later the jubilant mood turned somber when Sergeant Floyd died from what was probably appendicitis.

In late September the men met their first hostile Indians, the Teton Sioux. "These are the injuns to watch," an old trapper had warned them. "They extract the gold from your teeth if you ain't careful. And they ain't gonna let you get by 'em, neither, 'less you pay 'em a toll."

Captain Lewis offered the leader, Black Buffalo, coats and tobacco, and the chief gave the explorers painted buffalo skins and entertained them with food and dancing. Then he told Captain Lewis, "You can go back down the river or you can stay with us. But you cannot go past this point in the river."

The shoreline was suddenly alive with Sioux warriors, their arrows pointed straight at the men on the boat.

"Make ready for a fight," Captain Lewis told his men.

John was already loading his Kentucky rifle. Calmly, he knelt by a barrel of flour and waited.

Sergeant Ordway yanked the cover off the swivel gun. Private Shannon poured nearly a keg of nails down its barrel. Captain Clark lit a match and held it above the cannon. John knew that if Captain Clark touched the match to the cannon, they were to begin firing.

At about that time, Black Buffalo decided that he had enough coats and tobacco, after all. He waved the boats through.

"He'll send runners to other villages along the river," John told Captain Clark. "He'll tell them about the big gun. We won't have any trouble from the Indians up-river."

It was not Indians but nature that gave the corps its next problem. As the trees along the river dropped their gold and mahogany-red leaves, game became harder to find.

"We should save and tan the skins from now on," John said. "And any extra meat we must dry and keep for when we can't find any at all."

"We are not far from the Mandan Indian village," Captain Lewis said. "That's as far as the Spaniards got. We will hole up there for the winter."

Near the Mandan village the men cut tall, straight pine trees and built a three-sided fort. They would stay there until spring. They cut firewood and stored it inside the fort. During the long, cold months, John and the other hunters did their best to find food for everyone, but sometimes there wasn't enough. The Indians showed them how to keep from starving by eating tree bark.

Captain Lewis brought out his medicine kit often. He doctored frostbite, burns, and cuts. Mostly the men had to stay inside by the fire.

One evening John was on guard duty when two fur-wrapped figures approached. It was a trapper and his pregnant Indian wife. John led the two of them to the fire, and they warmed themselves as they talked with Captain Lewis and Captain Clark.

"I am Toussaint Charbonneau, and this is my wife, Sacagawea. We come offering our services in exchange for passage with you upriver."

"And what services can you give us?" Captain Lewis wanted to know.

"My father was French Canadian, but my mother was Shawnee. I speak her language. My wife is Shoshone — some call them the Snake people. She wants to go to her people."

Sacagawea, who seemed to John not far past her childhood, spoke to her husband in Shoshone.

"My wife says that for some of your journey you'll need horses. Her tribe has many horses for trade. She will speak on your behalf."

The captains agreed to let the Charbonneaus join them. One evening, while sleet whispered through the bare branches outside the fort, Sacagawea gave birth to a boy, Jean Baptiste Charbonneau. The baby was called Pomp, which was Shoshone for "firstborn."

John admired the brave Indian woman, who rarely spoke and seemed never to complain. Her husband, on the contrary, was quarrelsome and difficult, and John kept a cautious eye on him.

It was spring before they resumed their journey. They had traveled more than three months before Sacagawea

recognized several landmarks; they were close to the summer camp of her people. Captain Lewis, John, Droulliard, and Potts went to look for the Shoshone.

The men ran into a hunting party. The Indians scattered behind bushes and rocks.

"They think we're Blackfeet," Captain Lewis said. "Take off your shirts. Show them your white skin."

The men laid down their weapons and did as the captain had ordered. The Shoshone had never seen white skin before; they knew these men weren't their enemies. "A woman waits for you. She speaks your language," Captain Lewis said. Charbonneau translated for him.

York was waiting with Sacagawea, Clark, and the others. Hours before, the Indians hadn't known there were white men. Now they saw a black man. "Do men come in other colors, too?" one asked Captain Lewis.

Sacagawea's face suddenly burst into a smile. "Cameahwait!" she shouted in Shoshone, rushing to the leader. "I am your sister, Sacagawea!"

By accident and good luck, the corps had brought the woman to her very own brother. Cameahwait celebrated with a feast. He gladly traded horses to the corps.

Then Sacagawea surprised everyone. She agreed to go with the corps to its final destination, the Pacific Ocean, and rejoin her tribe on the return trip. Her baby and quarrelsome husband would accompany her.

Four

GOING HOME— BUT NOT QUITE

WHEN HE FIRST joined the Corps of Discovery, John Colter had believed that he was fairly woods-smart. Maybe he had been for the almost civilized woods and mountains of Virginia and Kentucky. But when it came to coping with the land he'd seen on this trip, he'd been as green as a new sapling.

Now he was satisfied that he'd become hickory hard. And he had seen what few men had seen. He'd witnessed firsthand the waves of the Pacific Ocean roaring like a mountain lion as they bore down on the rocky shore. They had sent sprays of foamy water high enough to douse him up on the cliffs. He'd seen squirrels that flew, mice that hopped, deer with ears as big as any mule's, and herds of

buffalo that were so great it took them all night to pass by. And he'd ridden rapids and been dashed against rocks like so much dandelion fluff. It was strange, holding all those pictures in his mind.

John's chest had swollen with pride just days before, as he'd watched Captain Clark carve evidence of their presence into a tall pine tree high above the water: his name, the date on which they'd first seen the ocean, December 3, 1805, and the words *By land from the U. States in 1804 and 5.*

They set up winter camp by the ocean and named the site Fort Clatsop. Then, on March 23, 1806, they turned the boats toward home. The return trip was a lot easier, as they were riding with the currents instead of against them. It seemed downright boring to John, whose taste for adventure exceeded even his gift of gab.

A couple of days west of the Mandan village the corps met up with two trappers, Joseph Dickson and Forrest Hancock, who were paddling upriver in search of more favorable hunting grounds. "While you fellows were spending your winter on the coast, we spent ours fairly comfortable with a band of Sioux," Dickson said.

"We sure did miss hearing English, though," Hancock added. "Maybe we oughta go on back with you a spell."

At the camp fire that night, the two men told of their trapping experiences. "Beaver's plentiful, and it's in big demand for hats back east," Dickson said. "If you can keep the Blackfeet from stealing the hairy bank notes out from under you, you can get plenty of money for the spring and fall ones."

"Right," Hancock said. "There ain't no point in trapping summer ones, though. Fur's too thin to bring much money."

John listened intently to the trappers. Eagerly he told them about everything he'd seen, too. "The more I think about going back to shoulder-to-shoulder people and buildings and noise, the better I like it here," he said.

"Reckon I'd forgot most of that. I don't really hanker to go back all that much. Why don't you stay here with us?" Dickson asked. "Take up trapping awhile."

John thought about it. When the corps reached the Mandan village on August 6, 1806, John approached Captain Lewis. "I'm not ready to go back, Captain. Winter's coming, and I want to hole up here if I can, do some trapping and exploring on my own. I figure to get me some beaver pelts and sell 'em at one of the blowouts in the spring down in Saint Louie."

A beaver was as shapeless as a sack of flour and weighed as much as a ten-year-old child. When a pelt was stretched over a hoop, it was three feet in diameter, as big as any wagon wheel. A stack of pelts as high as a rifle standing on its end would bring three or four dollars, as much as the rifle cost.

Captain Lewis nodded. "John, there hasn't been a job mean enough or dangerous enough that I haven't counted on you to do, no questions and no complaints. We brought you in as a hunter, yet you've willingly helped us lug boats over mountain passes no goat could conquer, you've eaten horse without a whimper when no other food was available, and you've faced down hostiles without blinking an eye. You're as rugged and smart as any man among us. I hereby release you from the Corps of Discovery and the U.S. Army. Your pay will be waiting for you in the Bank of Saint Louis whenever you're ready."

The corps gave the biggest blowout of the journey that night. Peter Cruzatte played the fiddle, and everybody stomp-danced and sang.

"One more story, John," Cruzatte begged when he set down his fiddle. "Just one more for the road."

It didn't take a whole lot of urging for John to agree. "Well, sir, there I was, trailing Old Ephraim—"

"Old Ephraim?" George Droulliard interrupted. "Who's that?"

John grinned. "Old Ephraim was an old pigeon-toed grizzly that had been pestering me for days. I decided to get me that ornery bear. I followed his tracks for a couple of hours. Then I came 'round an aspen tree only to find myself face to face with a moose with antlers as wide as a one-room cabin. That old moose turned on me—as you know, a moose's temper grows in proportion to the size of his antlers. Well, sir, he was one mad moose, and it was all I could do to outrun him and climb up a tree.

"I was a-sitting on that limb, a-panting from the run, when the tree commenced to shaking. That old moose was a-ramming his head against the tree, trying to shake me loose, I figured.

"I was a-hanging on for dear life, when what should I see sitting on that limb next to me but Old Ephraim, shaking as bad as I was."

"Then what, John?" Cruzatte asked. "Did you shoot Old Ephraim?"

John leaned back with his arms folded across his chest. "Well, the two of us just clung to each other while that old moose butted against the tree. Finally he gave that tree an extra good butt and knocked Old Ephraim clean out o' the tree. That bear fell on top of that moose and knocked the both of 'em out cold."

"Did you shoot 'em?" Cruzatte asked.

John frowned. "Course not! That wouldn't be honorable."

"Quit your joshing, John!" Cruzatte said. "Nobody's gonna believe a thing you say."

John smiled. "Can't help that. It's so, more or less."

John Colter hunted that fall of 1806 and spring of 1807 with Dickson and Hancock, but he didn't have the success he was expecting. Disappointed, and imagining himself homesick, John chopped down a tree and burned it hollow to make a dugout canoe, as he'd learned from the Indians. He loaded it with the pelts he had collected, and

after saying his farewells to his winter friends, he started down the Missouri toward Saint Louis.

The water ran swiftly—too swiftly for John. He wasn't *that* eager to get back to Saint Louis.

It seemed that at every bend in the river, John met a trader or trapper coming upriver, heading for the Rockies. Captain Lewis's report to President Jefferson must have made the West seem pretty attractive to the folks back home. The ripple of settlers swelled to a flood.

John felt a certain pride in having been there before these newcomers, having already seen it all, yet he envied them the experience of seeing it for the first time. His mind wandered as his dugout rode the current. What was beyond those trees? What was beyond the rivers? How far did the land go? What was it like? He'd hunted along these shores, but there was much more land to see.

Near the mouth of the Platte River, John saw several boats coming toward him. Standing at the bow of the first one was a bull of a man, barking instructions to the others as they strained with poles to push the boats forward.

The man waved to John and asked him to pull over. John moored his boat. The polemen guided the other boat next to his. While a couple of the men set up a camp fire and brewed some coffee, the leader spoke to John. "I am Manuel Lisa," he said. "I own a fur company and I'm going to set up a trading post."

John introduced himself.

"I have heard of you," Lisa said. "I could use your

experience with the Indians, especially the Crow and the Shoshone."

"I've traded with both tribes for horses," John said. "And I'm friends with some Shoshone. There's Saca- gawea, whose brother was a chief last time I saw 'em. Her husband's French and Shawnee."

John studied the man's face. His eyes were dark and brooding under thick, heavy brows and a low forehead. John had heard of this Manuel Lisa from other trappers. He was noted for a stormy temper.

"We don't like him much," one of his men whispered to John when Lisa walked off to check the boats. "But he's good at trading with the Indians. He treats them fairly, and they trust him."

"And he can talk a coon out of a tree," a toothless trapper named Joshua added. "He doesn't always have money himself, but he sure knows how to talk it out of those fancy-dressed city folks back home that do."

The first one nodded. "And he takes care of our families while we're out here trapping and trading."

John listened to each of them as he drank his coffee. He respected any man who dealt honestly with the Indians and took care of families. He'd have no trouble getting along with this fiery-tempered man, he thought. He spoke to Lisa. "To tell you the truth, I'm not so anxious to get back to civilization, anyway. I'll work for you, at least for a year."

John turned his boat around and followed Lisa upstream to where Lisa had decided to set up a permanent trading post. Standing lodgepole pines side by side to make a thick, high fence, the men built a post on the Yellowstone River at the mouth of the Bighorn River. Manuel Lisa named it Fort Raymond, after his son.

That settled, John filled his "possibles" sack, a leather pocketbook for ammunition, tools, and tobacco, and re-hung it on his belt. He packed a couple of horses with gifts to the Indians from Lisa. He took little jerky because he knew the woods were full of food. Lisa had said he was now something like a diplomat and traveling salesman, and his territory was the entire northwestern United States.

John knew that the Flatheads and the Shoshone lived on the other side of the Rockies, where there were no buffalo. Both tribes were plenty scared of running into the Blackfeet, but when they got hungry enough, they'd cross over the mountains and hunt on the plains. He figured he'd run into them somewhere on the plains, then talk their leaders into trading with Manuel Lisa at Fort Raymond.

John had been traveling the plains at a pretty steady pace when he noticed a reddish glow to the clouds, a reflection of camp fires. The following day he found a scattering of teepees. Some of the women at the camp were smoking buffalo meat, while others were tanning hides. Indian children squealed and ran about, playing some kind of tag. John recognized the pictures on the teepees, two different kinds. He was in luck! He had run into a couple of bands of Flatheads and Crows on a hunt. They probably figured that together they might be able to withstand an attack by Blackfeet.

John rode into camp. He held his right hand palm out in greeting to assure them that he was a friend. He dismounted and waited. That was a thing he'd learned about the Indians: You had to be patient; you couldn't rush them without destroying their trust.

Soon an older man, flanked by two men about John's age, stepped out of a teepee. He was joined by another older man wearing the traditional garb of the Flatheads.

John greeted them. He pulled a wad of tobacco from his possibles sack, offering it to them. A chief nodded, and one of the men fetched the pipe. John, the chiefs, and the braves sat in a circle and passed the pipe, each taking a puff on it. Men who had smoked the peace pipe together could then talk as friends.

John had just begun to tell the chiefs about Lisa's trading post when he heard shouting outside. A brave burst through the tent opening with the news: Blackfeet were attacking.

Five

FOREVER FRIENDS, FOREVER ENEMIES

JOHN GRABBED HIS long rifle and the sack with his ammunition. The women were herding the children and horses into the woods, and the braves were snatching up their **bows**, arrows, and spears.

John scrambled alongside the braves into a small thicket of trees and waited. He knew he wouldn't stand a chance with the murderous Blackfeet if he was caught. They hadn't been too fond of white intruders in the first place. Then Captain Lewis had shot one in a skirmish, ending any chance of ever making peace with them. They had sworn to kill all white men.

It looked as if the entire Blackfoot nation were racing toward them on their horses. Whooping and yelling some-

thing fierce, they shot one arrow after the other, until the trees were so riddled with arrows that they looked like porcupines.

John loaded and fired again and again. Suddenly, pain shot through his leg and he cried out. He'd been hit. He sat on the ground, willing himself not to think about his wound. Quickly, his experienced fingers loaded and fired his rifle.

The Crow and Flathead braves continued to fling their arrows toward the Blackfeet until at last the raiders retreated. Although greatly outnumbered, the two tribes had fended off the fierce Blackfeet. And John Colter, despite his wound, had stayed at their sides, fighting with them.

The women came with salves and prayer chants. The medicine man came. They doctored John and they bandaged him. They wrapped him in a blanket, and although he protested loudly, they took away his buckskin breeches.

When one of the women returned them, he saw that she had mended the tear made by the arrow. John thanked her for her kindness, then went to see the chiefs. "As we were saying . . ."

The chiefs smiled. One said, "You fought bravely by our sides, John Colter. You are truly a friend. We will trade with your Manuel Lisa."

John continued on his trip, seeking out Indians and getting them to agree to trade their furs for tobacco and rifles and horses.

For long periods of time John did not see anyone at all. He rode through stands of aspen and through the cutting prickly pear cactus. Sometimes he would see signs that someone had been there before.

At one point John decided to change the direction in which he had been riding. His horse seemed a bit hesitant and skittish, but the ground appeared reasonably flat, so John pushed him forward.

Bloop, blop. Ploop!

The horse backed up and did a little hopping jig, whinnying. John looked at the ground. What was going on?

Bloop, blop. Ploop!

John got off his horse and eased forward.

Bloop, blop. Ploop!

John jumped back. "Huh?" He'd seen a lot of things in his life, but he'd never seen the likes of this! It was a mud hole, gurgling and blistering and burping as if it were boiling.

John reached out his hand. He felt heat. It was a boiling mud hole! There was no place for a fire, but it was cooking all the same. Why, it was the devil's own cooking pot! And it wasn't the only one. There were others scattered about, busily boiling.

Cautiously, John led his horse through the area, where he saw many more of the mud pots. In other places there were cracks in the ground, from which steam hissed up. His jaw dropped as he stared in awe.

John continued to edge forward, looking in every direction, trying each step before he put his weight down for fear the ground might open up and suck him into the devil's house. What else could explain all this? he wondered.

Suddenly he saw a rush of water, like a waterfall moving in reverse. The water shot into the air as high as a tree. *P-tuuuiii!* It spit a fist-sized rock that rolled toward John, stopping at his feet.

"I swear, if this thing hasn't gone and laid an egg," John said. He reached down to pick it up; it was too hot. The water stopped spewing from the hole, but a cloud of steam remained hovering above it.

John had to be sure about what he was seeing. He made his camp right then and there and sat, waiting for it to happen again. Finally the water erupted. All through the night and into the next day, the water hissed and gurgled and steamed like a pot of boiling water, then would spew forth from the hole, leaving the air filled with steam. Sometimes it spit out another rock.

Maybe Indians had seen this before, but John was certain that no other white man had ever seen it, or he would have heard about it. This was something to tell about around camp fires.

John continued his travels in search of tribes willing to trade with Manuel Lisa. Once during his trek through what was to become Yellowstone National Park, he stopped and blazed a tree with an *X*, then initialed it, *JC*. In 1808 he carved his whole name on a rock and dated it. "Maybe someday people will find these and know that John Colter once passed this way," he said aloud.

Later, at Three Forks, near the Mandan village where John had first met Sacagawea and her husband, John was mulling over all that he had seen while his stew of hare and wild roots cooked. He heard a rustle in the brush and grabbed his rifle, ready to defend himself.

"John Colter!" someone said. The dark figure stepped into the light of the camp fire, and John saw that it was his old friend John Potts from the Corps of Discovery.

"Pull up a log and sit down," John said. "I have got something wondrous to tell you."

John Potts ate and listened to John with interest, nodding encouragingly. But when John had finished, John Potts only laughed. "You do tell 'em," he said. "And I think that's the best of all."

"But it's true!" John insisted.

"John, nobody believes a thing you say."

The two men hunted together for a few days and exchanged stories. On the third day they were deep in the woods when they were suddenly surrounded by a Blackfoot war party.

John's instinct was to reach for his trusty rifle. But there was only one shot in it, which meant they had two with Potts's rifle. And there were about twenty braves, maybe more in the bushes. They were doomed.

John Potts grabbed his gun and fired. The angry war party shot many arrows at him. As John was to tell it later, "he was made a riddle of."

The braves' leader stared at John. John looked back at him, square in the eyes, the same way he'd faced everything in his life.

"Can you run fast?" the brave asked John in sign language.

John knew he could run fast, but he shook his head. What was up? he wondered.

They made John take off his buckskins. They took away his moccasins. Then the leader made a sign like a running deer. John understood. They wanted him to run, then they would chase him. They wanted to make sport of him.

The leader showed John through sign language that he would drop a moccasin. When it hit the ground, John should run.

John nodded. He turned his back to his foes, but he looked over his shoulder at the moccasin. It hit the ground. Swift as a deer, John leaped over logs and dodged branches. He kept running, his bare feet sometimes coming down on prickly cactus thorns. Pain shot through him.

Behind him he heard shouts as the men kept pace with him. He pushed himself harder. His chest and his legs hurt, but he kept going.

Some of the shouting stopped. Maybe they would get tired before he did. He ran until he could hear only one shout behind him. Wouldn't that brave ever give up?

John's lungs ached, and his head throbbed painfully. How could he go on? But he had to. Blood trickled from his nose from his running so long and hard. It ran down his chest. He knew he had to look strange, naked and covered with blood. Maybe that was his chance!

John hoped he was right. He threw his hands into the air and spun around to face the lone brave. "Ay-eeeeeeeee!" John shouted.

The startled brave skidded to a stop, tripping over his spear. Quickly John grabbed the spear and pinned the brave to the ground. He could see in the distance that the war party was gathering again. Soon they would come after him. He was too tired to keep running.

John knew he had a little time before they could catch up. The Platte River was near. If he could make it across the river, maybe they would lose his trail.

John reached the river. He looked back. They were running his way. Soon they would reach him. John spotted some reeds along the water. There was a jam of logs, too, that had broken away from the shore and fallen in. John had an idea. He snapped off a reed. Just as he thought, it was hollow. Maybe his plan would work. If it didn't, he would have to run for it again.

Six

YET ANOTHER CHALLENGE

JOHN DOVE INTO the water. He swam under the jam of logs. He put one end of the hollow reed in his mouth. The other end he left sticking out of the water. He took a breath through the reed. It worked!

Soon John could hear the war party at the riverbank. The water churned as the braves hopped back and forth on the logs above his head, muttering among themselves. He hoped that no one would snap his reed—he would have to come up for air and would be discovered for sure.

John waited and waited, but they would not leave. Oh, no! John thought. They were setting up camp right there by his hiding place.

The water had turned cool. His muscles ached, and it

was hard to breathe through the reed for such a long time. When darkness closed in at last, John quietly surfaced between the logs. The camp fire was burning. Most of the braves were asleep, but several were still watching the water.

What if they decided to stay there for several days? John knew he had to make a move. As quietly as a fish, he swam under the water as far as he could, holding his breath. When he surfaced, he could still see the camp fire at a bend in the river.

John looked at the sky. The location of the full moon and the evening star meant that Fort Raymond would be east, right across the prairie. If he traveled by night and hid in the grass by day, maybe he could put some distance between himself and the war party. Maybe he could make it to the fort.

Every muscle in his body ached, and he was bruised and cut from his encounters with prickly pear cacti and stones. His belly cried out for food. Deer and rabbits were everywhere, but he had no rifle. He had no spear. He found a plant the Indians called breadroot and feverishly dug at the roots, cramming them into his mouth. He chewed cactus leaves for moisture. And he kept moving.

For seven chilling nights, John walked east. For seven searing days he cringed in the shade of anything he could find.

On the eighth night, the moon cast a silvery glow across

a jagged line of trees. But, no, they were not trees. They were the lodgepole-pine logs that formed the fence around the fort. He had made it!

John half stumbled and half crawled toward the gate of Fort Raymond. He tried to shout for help, but his throat was too dry and his tongue too swollen. He could only whimper.

Then shouts erupted from the fort. "Look! There's someone out there!"

The gates swung open, and men rushed to carry John inside. They brought him water, and he drank greedily, splashing some on his blistered face.

One by one, he called the men by name, and they stared at him, puzzled, until finally he shouted, "It's me, John Colter!"

The long trek had taken its toll on John; not even his friends recognized him. John rested and ate and regained his strength. And he stayed one more year, working for Manuel Lisa.

During that time, John Colter faced Blackfeet once more. While checking some of his animal traps, he was surprised by a war party. They immediately surrounded him.

John listened as the Blackfoot braves argued over his fate. He had learned enough of their language to understand what they were talking about.

"This man is like a ghost," one of them said. "He keeps coming back."

"Let's kill him with his own firestick," another suggested. "That way we will be sure." They forced John to load his rifle.

John had an idea. He measured the gunpowder in his palm and poured it into the barrel. He got a patch and a ball. He unsnapped the ramrod from the side of the rifle. But instead of pushing the ball into the barrel, he only pretended to do so. Keeping the ball in his hand, hidden between his fingers, he gave the rifle to the leader.

The Indian aimed the rifle at John's heart and fired. *Bam!* The powder flashed in the pan.

John snatched at the air, then opened his fingers to show them that he held the ball. The Indians stared, open-mouthed, for a moment. Then the leader threw down the rifle and they all ran away. John Colter was indeed a hard ghost to kill.

Back at Fort Raymond John told Manuel Lisa, "I have been shot once, captured twice, and chased until I dropped. I reckon I used up my last bit of luck. I'm going home."

It took John thirty days to get back to Saint Louis by dugout canoe. Saint Louis was known to the Indians as Red Head's Town because Captain Clark lived and worked there. John went to see him. He told him about all the things he had seen.

As John stood beside the map on the wall and spoke, the captain traced his trail on the map with a pen. He

labeled it John Colter's Trail. The area of the boiling mud pots he called Colter's Hell.

Although Captain Clark had believed John's stories, when John told others about the water leaping to the sky, the pots of boiling mud, and the steam spewing through cracks in the ground, they would merely shake their heads. "Oh, John," they would respond, "nobody believes a thing you say."

Angry at the doubters, John Colter began to exaggerate these stories, too. The logs became a dam belonging to a family of friendly beavers who had hidden him while the Indians walked overhead. And the wondrous geysers became fishing holes where he caught cooked fish.

John married an Indian woman and farmed for three years in La Charrette, Missouri, where his hero Daniel Boone lived. In 1813 John fell ill and died of jaundice. Although he was only thirty-eight when he died, John Colter had been to the Pacific Ocean and back—he had helped to launch the continentwide expansion of the United States. Three times he had denied the Blackfeet his scalp, and he had seen and done more than most people could do in two lifetimes.

"Whether any man believes me or not, I have seen wondrous things," he told his wife. "And the stories I've told are true—more or less."

Although eighteen years later William Sublette was credited with discovering the geysers and mud pots, the truth eventually came out. In the late 1880s John Colter's blazed tree was discovered. And in 1931 a potato farmer in Idaho unearthed a rock on which was carved *John Colter 1808.*

Thanks to his old friend Captain Clark, who always believed John, a peak in the southeast part of Yellowstone National Park is named for John Colter. And the trail forever bears his name. Some say that if you listen carefully to the steam hissing through the cracks in the ground, it whispers his name.

All this is true—more or less.

JOHN COLTER
ca. 1775–September 1813